CW00517209

Veronica Red

Crystal in the Night

— MOON CHILD —

Copyright © 2019 by Veronica Red. 783910

ISBN: Softcover   978-1-7960-0389-5
        EBook   978-1-7960-0388-8

All rights reserved. No part of this book may be
reproduced or transmitted in any form or by
any means, electronic or mechanical, including
photocopying, recording, or by any information
storage and retrieval system, without permission in
writing from the copyright owner.

This is a work of fiction. Names, characters, places
and incidents either are the product of the author's
imagination or are used fictitiously, and any
resemblance to any actual persons, living or dead,
events, or locales is entirely coincidental.

Print information available on the last page

Rev. date: 06/18/2019

To order additional copies of this book, contact:
Xlibris
1-800-455-039
www.xlibris.com.au
Orders@Xlibris.com.au

For my crystal children, Samuel and Riley

As the sun goes down, the stars return to the night.

Within the darkness, they shimmer and sparkle so bright.

Watching this magic warms my heart with so much love,

Sitting on my own here, just me and the universe above.

Today is a new moon, a time of new beginnings.

Even though I can't see her, I can feel her energy brimming.

Like a crystal in the night sky, always pleasing to the eye,

There is still much more to understand, to learn and clarify.

Here and now is the perfect time to make a new vow

To flow along with the changing moon, symbolising this journey with a bow.

I'm out here again; now three days have passed.

First step is to write down everything for which I have asked.

A beautiful crescent is now visible in the night sky.

It's the symbol of the new beginning, and to the old, I now say goodbye.

Moon is appearing lighter and brighter now that four new days have passed.

Powerful energies have increased; things I've asked for are now well broadcast.

It has been easy learning to create paths that are new.

The trick, however, is ensuring there is firm action too.

As the moon's light grows, it is now at first quarter,

With the sun illuminating half the moon, the other hidden, still out of order.

The moon is now at waxing gibbous stage.

She is fuller and brighter, more alive with each passing day.

Just like the increasing glow of the powerful moon,

All my intentions are fine-tuned and preparing to bloom.

At this phase, we take a glimpse of the very next level.

All the lessons and clarity will be displayed as the night crystal.

Three magical days have passed; the moon is so full and round.

Completely mesmerised by her transformation, it's been such a turnround.

In the beginning, whilst in the darkness, I made a vow with a bow,

To now see this completion, celebrating this moment here and now.

This spectacular sight with the night sky so clear,

We can enjoy the abundance of the full moon twelve to thirteen times a year.

As another four days have gently passed,

Releasing and letting go have happened at long last.

Sharing my gratitude and feeling the benefits of all I have learned,

It's now a time when I give back to all who have followed my journey in return.

As a gift, I wish to share this view with my audience, which is you,

To watch the bright moon slowly fade, together seeing the revealing preview.

The moon is now at last quarter stage, the cycle beginning to end.

All my old thoughts are now clearing away with the help of my universal friend.

Having been so attuned to my outer world has taken me away

From my desire to reconnect with my innermost self and no longer stray.

The beautiful moon phases have helped me decide my next step

And be hopeful of the returning cycles of my new footsteps.

Four days have passed; our crystal in the night is now a dimmed light.

Stepping outside, very comfortable in the darkness with this delightful sight.

Resting, preparing for rebuilding into a new phase, are being felt.

Just as this moon cycle, being gentle with myself all for good health.

We only have one moon; the same moon is here every single night.

Peace is there in the darkness, nothing to fear in this glorious twilight.

Our beautiful moon reflects the sunlight; depending on how much we see

Will tell a story of the position of the moon, sun, and earth like a family tree:

CPSIA information can be obtained
at www.ICGtesting.com
Printed in the USA
BVHW090955240619
551795BV00002B/36/P

* 9 7 8 1 7 9 6 0 0 3 8 9 5 *